Super-Duper Science

Incredible Insects!

by Annalisa Suid
illustrated by Marilynn G. Barr

For Greg & Tara

Publisher: Roberta Suid
Copy Editor: Carol Whiteley
Design & Production: Santa Monica Press
Cover Art: Mike Artell
Educational Consultant: Tanya Lieberman

Also by the author: *Save the Animals!* (MM 1964), *Love the Earth!* (MM 1965), *Learn to Recycle!* (MM 1966), *Sing A Song About Animals* (MM 1987), and *Preschool Connections* (MM 1993).

On-line address: MMBooks@AOL.com

P.O. Box 1680, Palo Alto, CA 94302

1-878279-89-0

Recycled paper

Printed in the United States of America

987654321

Contents

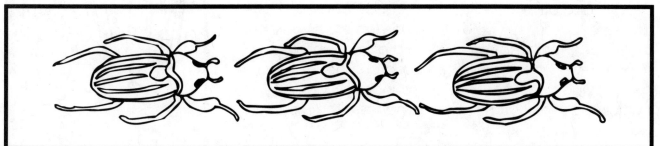

Introduction: Why Insects?

Insects are talented (mosquitoes can beat their wings 300 times a second!), famous (ever hear of Jiminy Cricket in Disney's "Pinocchio"?), musical (cicadas sound as harmonious as an orchestra), and all-around incredible!

Your students will learn about the exciting insect world (and spider world, too) while practicing writing, reading, research, performance, and speaking skills. They'll give many-legged reports, speak like insects, hold buggy spelling "bees," chart an average insect's family tree, star in a musical review . . . and much more. Most of the activities can be simplified for younger students or extended for upper grades. This book will enhance learning in many subjects through exploration of the exciting insect world.

Incredible Insects! is divided into four parts and a resource section. Through hands-on activities, **Hands-On Discoveries** will help answer science questions such as, "What does a butterfly baby look like?" or "What's it like inside a cocoon?" Reproducible sheets with a special ladybug icon have directions written specifically for the children.

Nonfiction Book Links features speaking, writing, and reporting activities based on nonfiction resources. Most activities are accompanied by helpful handouts, which will lead children through the research procedure. When research is required, you have the option of letting children look for the facts needed in your classroom, school, or local library. Or use the "Super-Duper Fact Cards" located in the resource section at the back of this book. These cards list information for 16 insects (and other creepy crawlies). You can duplicate the cards onto neon-colored paper, laminate, and cut them out. Then keep the cards in a box for children to choose from when doing their research. These cards also provide an opportunity for younger children to participate in research projects. The research is provided for them on easy-to-read cards.

The **Fiction Book Links** section uses chapter books and storybooks to introduce information about interesting insects, spiders, and centipedes. This section's activities, projects, and language extensions help children connect with fictional insects. Each "Link" also includes a tongue twister. You can challenge children to create their own twisters from the insect facts they've learned. Also included in this section are decorating suggestions for "setting the stage" for each particular book.

It's Show Time! presents new songs sung to old tunes and costume suggestions for putting on a performance. The songs can be duplicated and given to the children. If you want to hold a performance, write each performer's name on the reproducible program page and pass copies out to your audience.

Each of the first three sections ends with a "Super-Duper Project," an activity that uses the information children have learned in the unit. These projects include creating an insect, writing a famous bug story, and holding an awards ceremony. A choral performance is a possible "Super-Duper" ending for the "It's Show Time!" section.

All About Insects

True Insects

True insects have segmented body parts, front wings and back wings, six legs, and mouth parts that can pierce and suck. The body of an insect is divided into three parts: head, thorax, and abdomen. Insects have a hard covering on the outside of their bodies. This is a kind of skeleton that protects the soft insides.

Some insects live on dry land, while others live in or near water. Most insects eat by sucking plant juices. Some suck the blood of other insects and spiders. Others feed on humans and other animals.

__This__ is an insect.

Antennae

Six legs

Abdomen

Front wings

Hind wings

Insects include: ants, aphids, bees, beetles, butterflies, cockroaches, grasshoppers, flies, mosquitoes, moths, and wasps.

All About Insects

Spider Insights

Spiders are arachnids. Arachnids have four pairs of eyes, eight legs, no wings, and two body sections instead of three. A spider's eyes, legs, and jaws are on the front body part. The back part, which is much larger, has a set of little taps called spinnerets.

<u>This</u> is not an insect.

Four pairs of eyes

Eight legs

Arachnids include: scorpions, mites, and ticks.

Insect Camouflage Mural

Many insects use camouflage as a way to survive. Some catch their prey through this fancy fakery, while others avoid being eaten by disguising themselves. For example, the day-flying zygaenid moth from Southeast Asia is not poisonous, but birds keep away because of its coloring (red, yellow, and black), which means "poisonous" in the wild.

Materials:
"Fancy Faking" Hands-on Handout (p. 9), "Butterfly Pattern" (p. 10), crayons (including red, yellow, and black), markers, glitter, glue, scissors, butcher paper, tempera paint, paintbrushes

Directions:
1. Discuss camouflaging with students. Many insects use camouflage for survival.
2. Duplicate the "Fancy Faking" Hands-on Handout and the "Butterfly Pattern" for each child.
3. Provide crayons, markers, glitter, and glue for children to use to decorate their butterflies. Encourage them to either camouflage their butterflies or color the insects with red, yellow, and black.
4. Have children cut out the patterns when they're finished.
5. Let children decorate a sheet of butcher paper to use as the background for their butterflies. They can paint the background to work with their chosen camouflage.
6. Post the completed mural on a wall in the classroom or hallway.
7. Have children post their butterflies all over the mural.

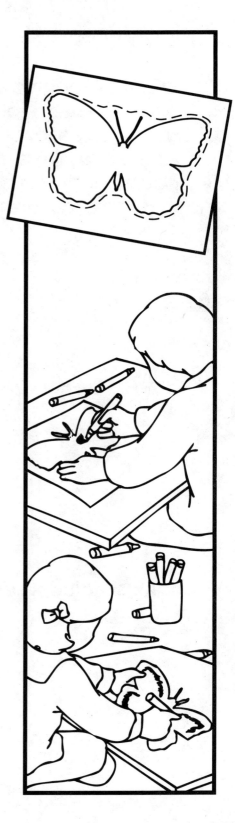

Fancy Faking

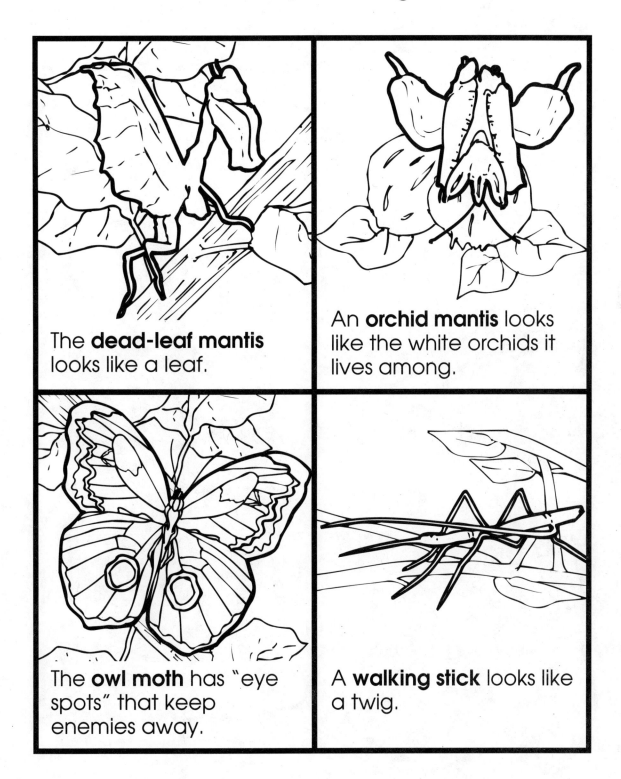

The **dead-leaf mantis** looks like a leaf.

An **orchid mantis** looks like the white orchids it lives among.

The **owl moth** has "eye spots" that keep enemies away.

A **walking stick** looks like a twig.

Butterfly Pattern

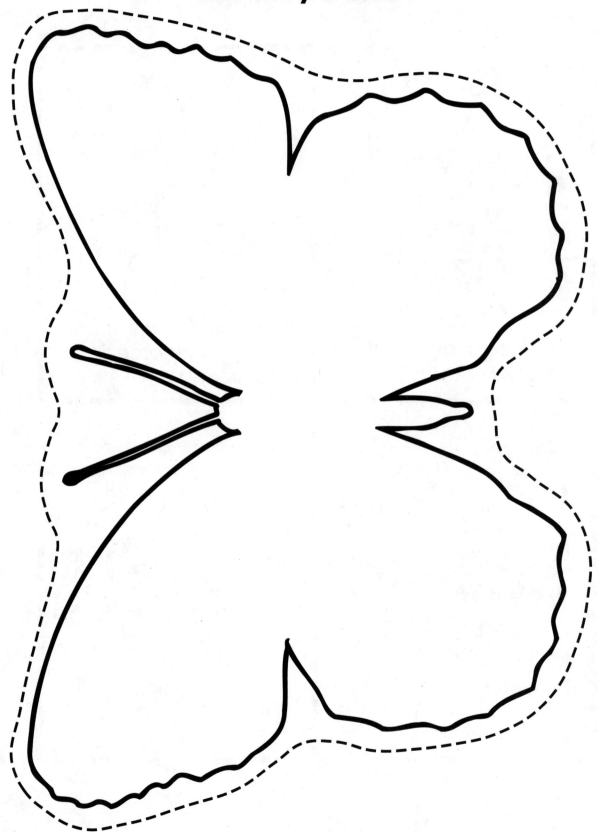

Moth Mix-Up

Moths protect themselves from predators through camouflage. During the Industrial Revolution, tree trunks changed color due to pollution. Light-colored moths, previously numerous, became nearly extinct, and black moths increased in number. After people worked to clean up the environment, the black trunks returned to their original color. When the white trunks reappeared, the white moths reappeared.

Materials:
"Moth Mix-Up" Hands-on Handout (p. 12), "Moth Pattern" (p. 13), scissors, glue or paste, construction paper (black and white), tape

Directions:
1. Make one copy of the "Moth Mix-Up" Hands-on Handout and the "Moth Pattern" for each child.
2. Have the children perform this pollution-based camouflage activity either singly or in small groups. (Directions for the activity are on the following page.)
3. Record the children's findings and have them share their discoveries with the rest of the class.

Option:
Do this activity as a class. Have children help you create paper tree trunks by fastening large sheets of black and white construction paper to a wall or bulletin board. Have children make two-sided moths in the same manner described on page 12. Let children take turns holding the moths up to the paper. Have the children discuss their findings together.

Moth Mix-Up

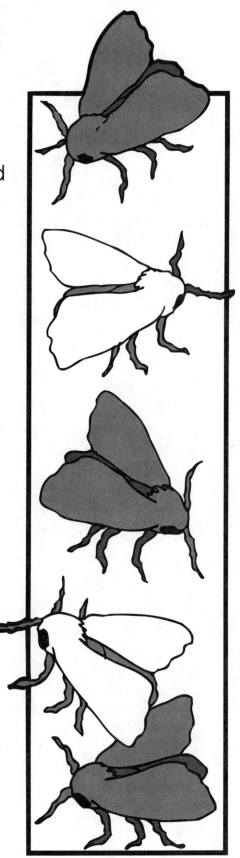

What You Do:
1. Glue or paste a white sheet of paper to a black sheet of paper.
2. Cut out moth shapes from the two-sided paper.
3. Hold the moths up to black and white sheets of construction paper.
4. Answer the questions below.

Questions:
1. Which color would hide black moths?

2. Which color would hide white moths?

3. Why would black moths survive better when trees were polluted?

Moth Pattern

Kid Cocoons

Cocoons are silk houses that some insects make for protection while they undergo metamorphosis. (See p. 18 and p. 20 for more on metamorphosis.) There are both small cocoons and large cocoons. Some cocoons are tightly woven, others fragile.

Materials:
Toilet paper

Directions:
1. Discuss cocoons with your children.
2. Have your students name insects that they think make cocoons. These include butterflies, caddis flies, sawflies, and bumblebees. The most commonly found cocoons are made by moths.
3. Divide children into pairs. Provide toilet paper rolls for children to take turns wrapping up in—make sure that only their bodies are covered, not their heads.
4. Have children lie down, close their eyes, and pretend that they are curled up tightly inside a cocoon. Describe what it feels like: safe, warm, dark. . . . Talk in a soft, soothing voice. Explain that while children went into the cocoon looking like a caterpillar, they will emerge looking like a butterfly, moth, bumblebee, etc.
5. Now have the children imagine that they are emerging from their cocoon. They should slowly unwrap (or break through) the toilet paper and very carefully stand up. Children pretending to be butterflies can spread their "wings," and then fold their arms together behind their backs. (Butterflies rest with their wings folded together.)
6. Make sure all children have a turn to play at being caterpillars.

Tissue Paper Beetles

Ladybugs have two sets of wings: a hard outer shell that is red with black dots (seven in common ladybugs), and a transparent set that the ladybug uses to fly. In ladybugs (and many other beetles), the front pair of wings has been transformed into tough wing covers. These are called elytra. A flying beetle must lift its elytra high enough to allow the wings beneath to unfold and to beat without interference.

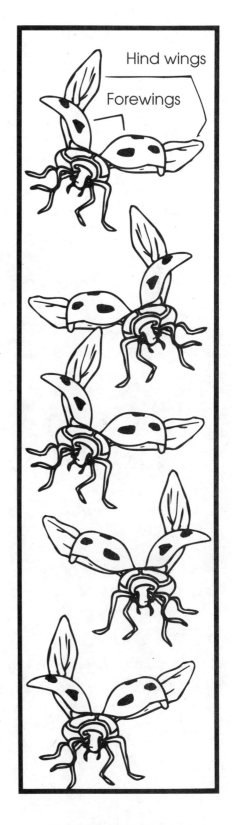

Materials:
"Two-Shelled Beetles" Hands-on Handout (p. 16), "Ladybug Patterns" (p. 17), heavy paper or oak tag, tissue paper squares (black and red), glue, clear cellophane or waxed paper, tape, scissors

Directions:
1. Duplicate a copy of the "Two-Shelled Beetles" Hands-on Handout for each child.
2. Duplicate the "Ladybug Patterns" onto heavy paper or oak tag. Make one for each child.
3. Children can scrunch up the black and red tissue paper squares and glue to the ladybug's shell.
4. Provide clear cellophane or waxed paper from which children can cut out their ladybug's "flying wings."
5. Children can use tape to make a "hinge" to attach their ladybug's elytra (wing covers) to the flying wings.
6. Have some beetle and ladybug books on display for children to read through.
7. Children can take their lucky ladybugs home.

Option:
Children can learn more about ladybugs by referring to the "Super-Duper Ladybug Fact Card" (p. 75).

Two-Shelled Beetles

What You Need: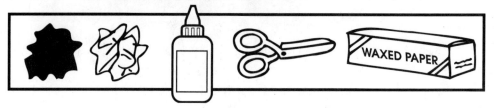

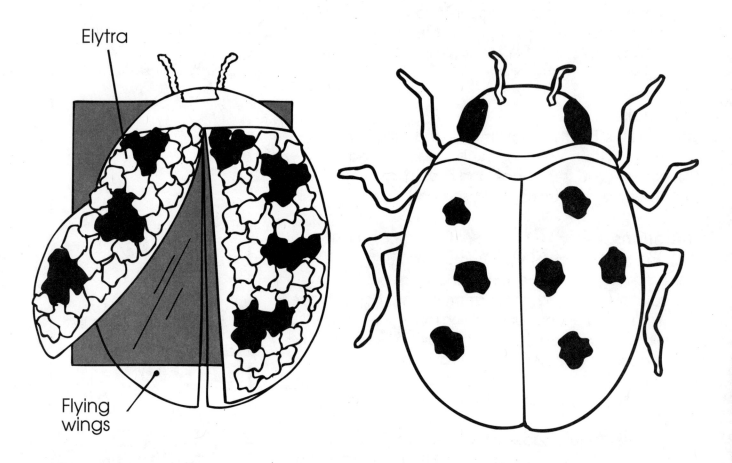

Elytra

Flying
wings

What You Do:

1. Cover the shell of your ladybug with red and black tissue paper. You can ball the paper up and glue the balls to the shell.
2. Use the wing pattern to cut out a set of wings from clear cellophane or waxed paper.
3. Attach the shell on top of the wings using a hinge of tape across the top.

Ladybug Patterns

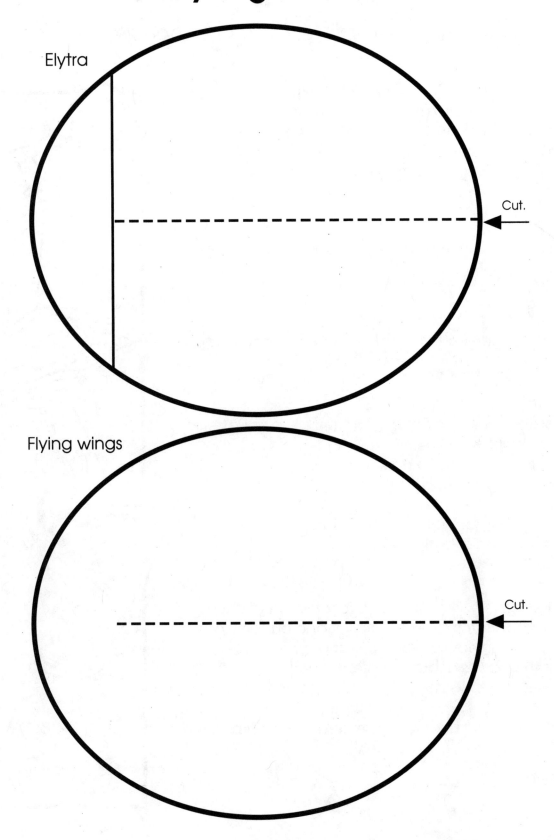

Elytra

Cut.

Flying wings

Cut.

Butterfly Babies
Complete Metamorphosis

Butterflies undergo complete metamorphosis, meaning a change of body form with stages (egg, larvae, and adult) that are distinct from each other. The adult butterfly does not resemble the caterpillar or pupal stages.

- The butterfly larva (caterpillar) is active in the larval stage.
- In its next stage it is called a pupa, and it is surrounded by a cocoon.
- When it emerges, it is an adult butterfly. This is complete metamorphosis.

Materials:
"Butterfly Babies Patterns" (p. 19), scissors, crayons or markers

Directions:
1. Duplicate one copy of the "Butterfly Babies Patterns" for each child.
2. Let the children cut out the patterns.
3. Provide crayons and markers for children to use to color the patterns.
4. Discuss the fact that the caterpillars look very different from the adult butterflies.

Option:
Provide Popsicle sticks and glue for children to use to make puppets from their caterpillar and butterfly patterns. They can hold up the correct puppets while you discuss the stages of butterfly life.

Note:
Other insects that undergo complete metamorphosis include ants, bees, and beetles.

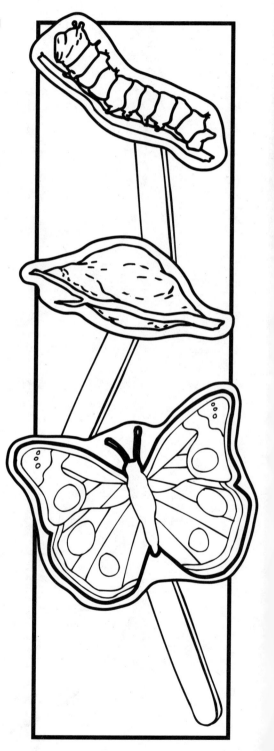

Butterfly Babies Patterns

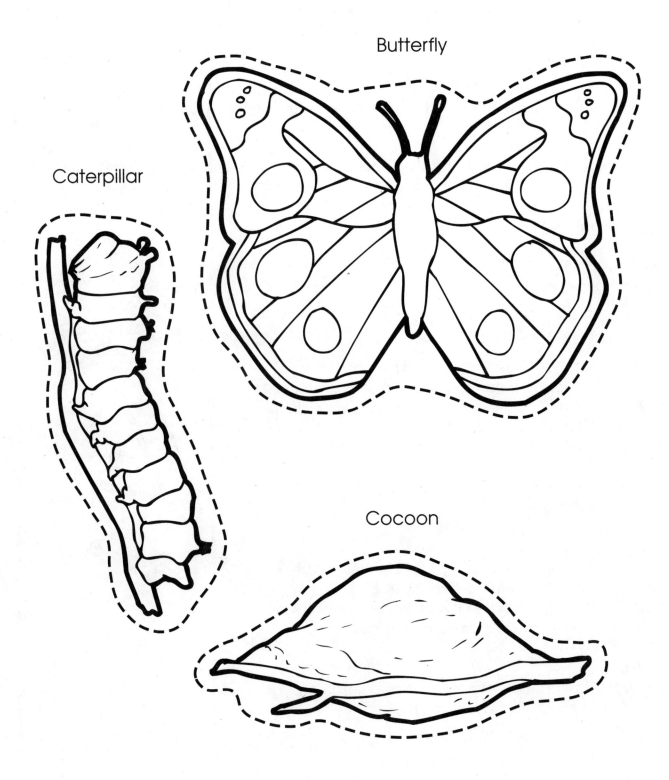

Butterfly

Caterpillar

Cocoon

How Grasshoppers Grow
Incomplete Metamorphosis

Unlike butterflies and many other insects, grasshoppers do not undergo complete metamorphosis. In incomplete metamorphosis, the insect looks like the adult when it is a nymph.

- Grasshoppers start as eggs.
- Nymphs hatch from the eggs. The nymphs are young grasshoppers. They look like smaller versions of grown-up grasshoppers.
- The final stage is the "adult" stage.

Materials:
"Grasshopper and Nymph Patterns" (p. 21), heavy paper, oak tag, scissors, crayons or markers

Directions:
1. Duplicate the "Grasshopper and Nymph Patterns" onto heavy paper or oak tag. Make one copy for each child.
2. Have children cut out the patterns.
3. Provide children with crayons or markers to use to decorate their patterns.
4. Discuss the fact that the nymphs look like smaller versions of the adult insects.

Option:
Provide Popsicle sticks and glue for children to use to make puppets from their grasshopper and nymph patterns. They can hold up the correct puppets while you discuss the stages of grasshopper life.

Note:
Other insects that undergo incomplete metamorphosis include aphids and stinkbugs.

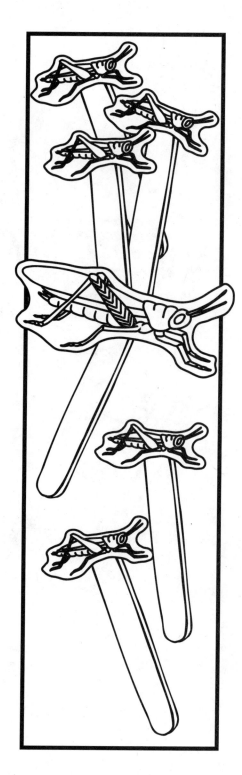

Grasshopper and Nymph Patterns

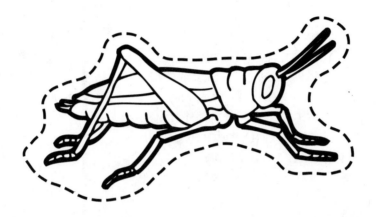

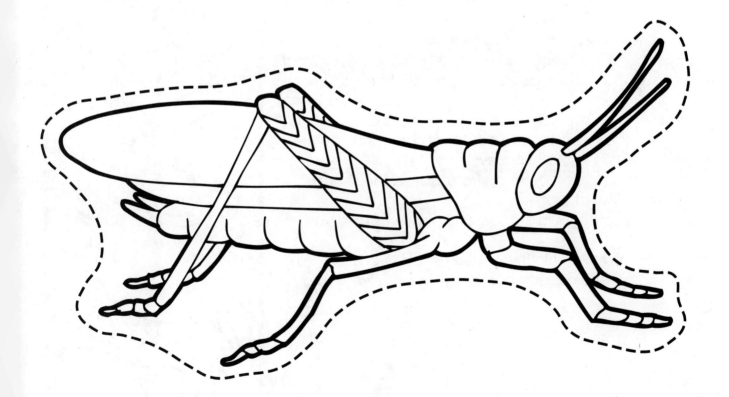

Create-a-Bug

Once the children have learned about insects, they can create their own from a variety of scraps, recyclables, and found objects.

Materials:

"All About Insects" Hands-on Handouts (pp. 6-7), "Create-a-Bug Patterns" (p. 23), recyclables (cardboard boxes, paper bags, toilet roll and paper towel tubes, lids, cartons), fabric and yarn scraps, glue, paste, construction paper, glitter, sequins, buttons, tempera paints, paintbrushes, clay or playdough, crayons or markers, leaves, twigs, wiggly eyes (optional)

Directions:

1. Duplicate the "All About Insects" handouts and the "Create-a-Bug Patterns" for each child.
2. Provide a variety of materials for children to use to create their own insects, spiders, or other creepy crawlies. Remind children to make sure their insects have the appropriate number of legs, wings, eyes, and so on. Children may also want to take into account whether their creatures will need to be camouflaged, or how else they might protect them from enemies.
3. Once the creatures are completed, let children help you set up an in-class display:
   - Flying bugs can be hung from clothesline strung across the classroom.
   - Crawling bugs can creep along shelves and counters.
   - Spiders might sit in the center of yarn webs.
4. Invite other classes to observe your creative display.

Create-a-Bug Patterns

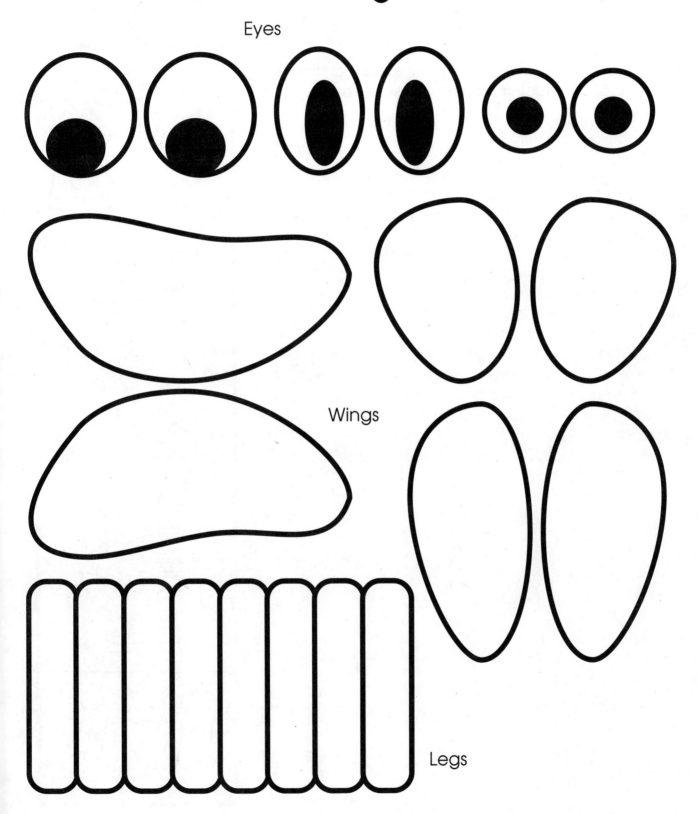

Eyes

Wings

Legs

Insect Glossaries

Materials:
"Insect Glossary" Hands-on Handout (p. 25), dictionaries, pencils, construction paper, stapler, crayons or markers

Directions:
1. Duplicate one "Insect Glossary" Hands-on Handout for each child. Explain that a glossary is a list of special words on a subject with definitions.
2. Have children look up each word in the dictionary.
3. Children should write the definition next to the word to create their own insect glossaries. Younger children can draw a picture.
4. As children learn new insect words (or phrases), have them add them to their glossaries.
5. Provide construction paper and a stapler for children to use to bind their pages together. They can decorate the cover of the book with insect drawings.

Option:
White-out the words and duplicate one page for each child. Let children write in their own insect-related words and definitions.

Insect Glossary

abdomen	
antennae	
cocoon	
larva	
segment	
thorax	

Centipede's Feet Report

Materials:
"Super-Duper Centipede Fact Card" (p. 72), one copy of the "Centipede's Feet" Hands-on Handout (p. 27) per child, pencils or markers

Directions:
1. Divide your students into groups of five or six.
2. Have the children brainstorm names for their groups, for example, Curious Centipedes, and so on. Tell them that a centipede is not an insect!
3. Each child in the group should learn two facts about his or her chosen centipede. (The children can present either one or two facts during the reports.) Children can either refer to the "Super-Duper Centipede Fact Card," or do research on their own using books in the library.
4. Children can record their facts and resource information on the "Centipede's Feet" Hands-on Handout.
5. Have children give reports to the class in their groups. The children in each group should stand with their arms on the waist of the child in front, creating the look of a centipede.

Options:
- Have each child in the class learn one fact about a centipede. Have the entire class link arms to waist to form one long centipede. Go to other classes and give centipede reports, beginning with the fact that the average centipede has 35 pairs of legs.
- Groups may want to coordinate their dress for the day of their report. For instance, they might all wear the same color shirt, socks, or pants.
- Trace around children's shoes onto sheets of construction paper. Have children write a fact inside their shoe pattern and cut out. Link these "Fact Feet" with paper clips and make a chain of feet. Or hang the "Fact Feet" from a clothesline strung across the classroom.

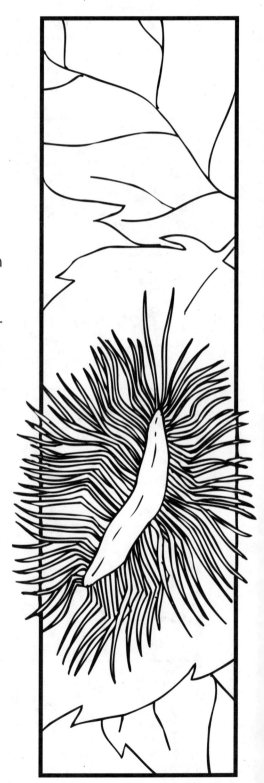

Centipede's Feet

Name: _____

Date: _____

Name of group: _____

Fact 1:

_____

_____

_____

Fact 2:

_____

_____

_____

Books I used:

Title: _____

Author: _____

Title: _____

Author: _____

Title: _____

Author: _____

Interview with an Insect

Materials:
"Insect A to Z List" (p. 78), "Insect Fact Sheet" Hands-on Handout (p. 29), "Insect Interview Sheet" Hands-on Handout (p. 30), pencils or markers

Directions:
1. In these reports, children research insects and then play the part of those insects in interview settings.
2. Let each child choose an insect to research from the "Insect A to Z List." Children can use the "Super-Duper Fact Cards" at the end of the book to research their insects. Or they can use books from the library.
3. Duplicate one copy of the "Interview with an Insect" handout and the "Interview Sheet" for each child.
4. Have the children research their chosen insect using the guidelines on the "Interview with an Insect" Hands-on Handout. Then have them write questions based on the facts using the "Interview Sheet" Hands-on Handout.
5. Once the children have finished their research, divide them into pairs. Have each partner take a turn interviewing the other in front of the class.
6. Set up an interview schedule, perhaps working through five to six interviews per day.

Options:
- Children can dress up to look like their chosen insects, for example, a child pretending to be a grasshopper could wear all green clothing.
- Interviewers can hold simple microphones (cardboard tubes with egg carton sections glued to the top).

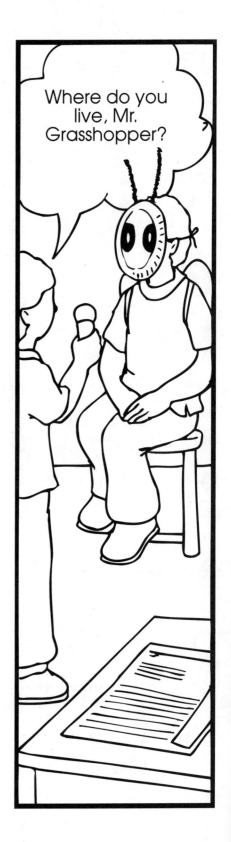

Insect Fact Sheet

Use this fact sheet to record at least four facts about your chosen insect. (Remember to list the books you used.) You can use the back of this sheet if you need more room.

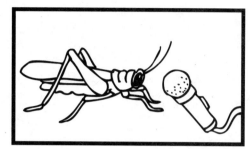

My name is: _____

My insect is: _____

Fact:_____

_____

Fact:_____

_____

Fact:_____

_____

Fact:_____

_____

Books I used:

Title: _____

Author: _____

Title: _____

Author: _____

Insect Interview Sheet

Write your answers under the questions. Write your own question for question 5. Your partner will use these questions to interview you in front of the class.

Question 1: What kind of insect are you?

_____

_____

Question 2: Where do you live?

_____

_____

Question 3: What enemies do you have?

_____

_____

Question 4: What do you eat?

_____

_____

Question 5:

_____

_____

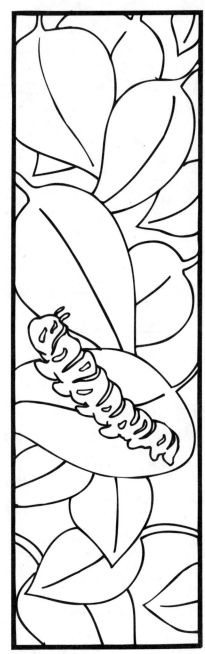

Bug Birth Announcements

Materials:

"Bug Birth Announcement" Hands-on Handout (p. 32), "Bug Birth Announcement Pattern" (p. 33), "Super-Duper Fact Cards" (pp. 70-77) or library books, crayons and markers, glitter, glue

Directions:

1. Challenge children to find out how many eggs a typical insect (of their choice) lays.
2. Duplicate the "Bug Birth Announcement" Hands-on Handout and have children research the answers to the questions on the sheet. They can research the information in books from the library, or use the "Super-Duper Fact Cards" at the end of this book.
3. Have the children make birth announcements for the bug of their choice using the "Birth Announcement Pattern." Provide crayons and markers, glitter, and glue for children to use to decorate the patterns.
4. Post the completed announcements on a bulletin board. Make sure that the top flap can be opened so that children can read the information within.

Bug Birth Announcement

What You Do:
1. Choose an insect (or spider) to research.
2. Answer the following:

• My insect or spider's name is: _____

_____

• My insect or spider has _____
eggs at a time.   (number of)

• When the babies hatch they are: (circle one)

        larva   nymphs   other

• This is what the egg looks like (draw a picture):

• This is what the baby looks like when it hatches
(draw a picture):

3. Use the "Bug Birth Announcement Pattern" to record the birth of the babies. List the type of babies, the number of babies born, the location of their birth (under a leaf, for example), and any other information you'd like.
4. Decorate the front of the card.

Bug Birth Announcement Pattern

(Draw a picture on front—then fold on dotted line.)

Mr. and Mrs. _____

(type of insect or spider)

are proud to announce the birth of

their _____ children. The babies

(number)

were born _____ .

(location)

Insect Family Trees

Materials:
Completed "Bug Birth Announcements" (p. 31), "Insect Family Tree" Hands-on Handout (p. 35), crayons or markers

Directions:
1. Discuss the concept of family trees.
2. Draw a simple family tree, perhaps your own, on the chalkboard. Show at least three generations: grandparents, parents, children.
3. Have the children use the information they researched in the "Bug Birth Announcement" activity for this project.
4. Children will use crayons or markers to chart two generations of bugs (or spiders) on the "Insect Family Tree" Hands-on Handout.
5. Post the completed family trees or bind them together in a classroom album.

Option:
If you post the "Insect Family Trees," cover the bulletin board first with green paper. Tape leaves to the border (or leaf shapes cut from orange and yellow construction paper).

Insect Family Tree

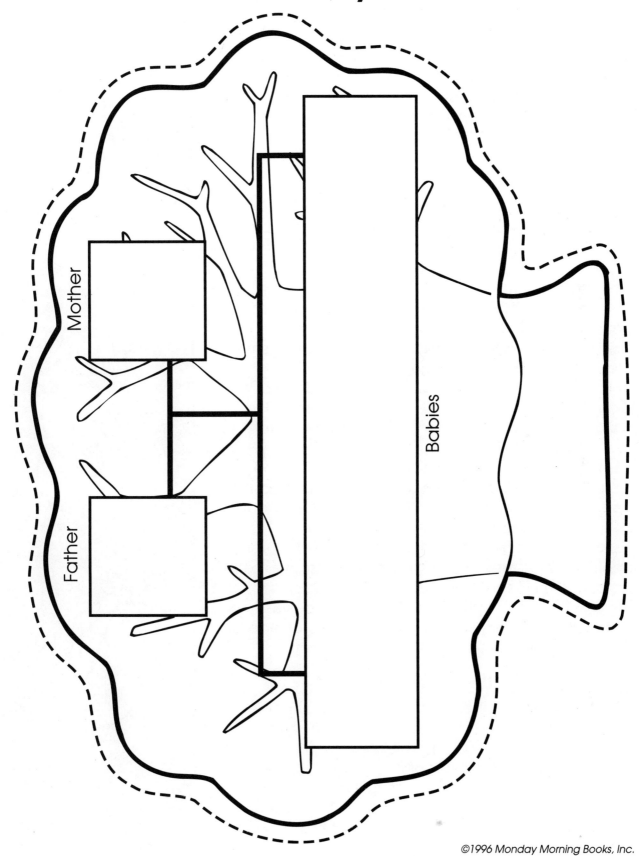

"Talking" Like Insects

Although insects use sight, sound, and touch to "talk," they rely mostly on their sense of smell. This sense is very highly developed in insects. For insects who are blind and deaf, like termites, smelling and touching are the only ways they can communicate.

Materials:

"'Talking' Like Insects" Hands-on Handout (p. 37), "Super-Duper Fact Cards" (pp. 70-77), one copy of the "Oral Report Sheet" Hands-on Handout (p. 38) per child

Directions:

1. Discuss the different ways that people communicate with each other: by phone, by fax, by speaking, by sign language, by yelling, by whispering, by tapping someone on the shoulder, by waving, and so on.
2. Now discuss the fact that human beings don't consciously use their sense of smell to communicate. However, this is the most important way that insects "talk" to each other.
3. Let children choose insects to research, using the "'Talking' Like Insects" Hands-on Handout. They can use the "Super-Duper Fact Cards" at the end of this book, or they can use library books for researching.
4. Have children give short (one to two minutes) oral reports in which they discuss their chosen insect's methods of communicating; they should also give examples of the way their creepy crawly gives and receives information. Children can prepare for their oral reports using the guidelines on the "Oral Report Sheet."

Options:

• Children can give their report in the manner of their chosen insect. If they researched a firefly, they can bring in a flashlight and dim the lights.
• Speakers can give the rest of the class a chance to talk like their chosen bug. For example, if a child researched a cricket, he or she can teach the class a few chirps, then host a cricket panel of chirping friends.

"Talking" Like Insects

Insects talk to each other in different ways.

A bee  dances

A firefly  flashes its lantern

A cricket  chirps

A spider  listens

A grasshopper  sings

A cockroach  makes noise

A butterfly  watches and smells

Oral Report Sheet

Answer the following questions:

- My insect's name is: _____

- My insect talks by: _____

_____

_____

_____

_____

_____

My insect's
name is

_____

Draw a picture of your insect, or trace
one from a book. Show this picture during
your report.

Spelling Bees

Materials:
"Spelling Bee Patterns" (pp. 40-41), "Hive Pattern"
(p. 42), crayons or markers, hat, scissors

Directions:
1. Duplicate the "Spelling Bee Patterns," making one
sheet for each child and a few extra sheets for teacher
use.
2. Color the "Hive Pattern," and post it on a bulletin
board. Cut out one extra set of bees and post them
around the hive.
3. Have children learn how to spell each word.
4. Host a spelling bee in your classroom. Keep one set
of bees in a hat and pull out one at a time, asking
each child in turn to spell the word on the bee. (Older
children will be able to give you both the spelling and
the definition that they have looked up.)
5. Continue with the spelling bee, having each child
who misspells a word sit down.

Options:
- Duplicate blank bees and let children write in their
  own insect-related words.
- Younger children can simply tape the bees to a
  sheet of writing paper and practice copying the
  words.

Spelling Bee Patterns

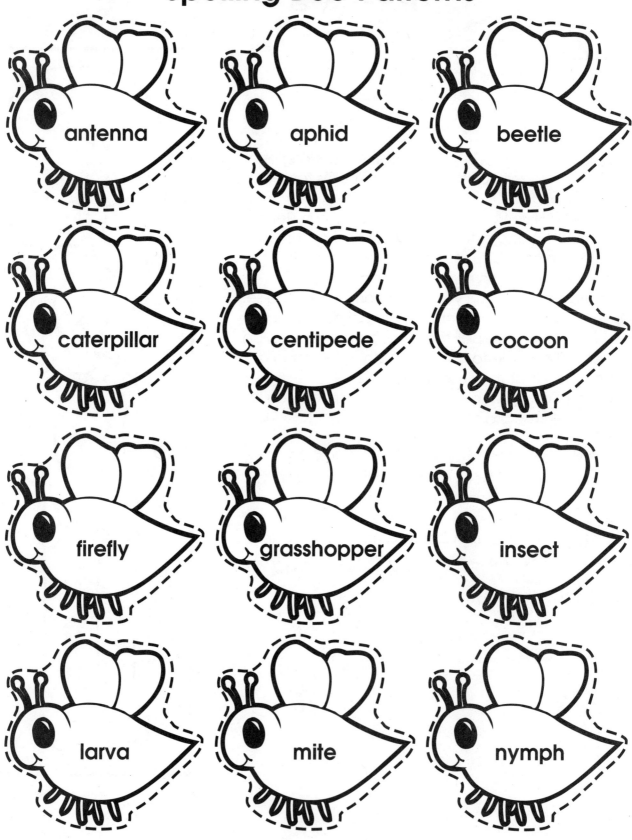

antenna

aphid

beetle

caterpillar

centipede

cocoon

firefly

grasshopper

insect

larva

mite

nymph

Spelling Bee Patterns

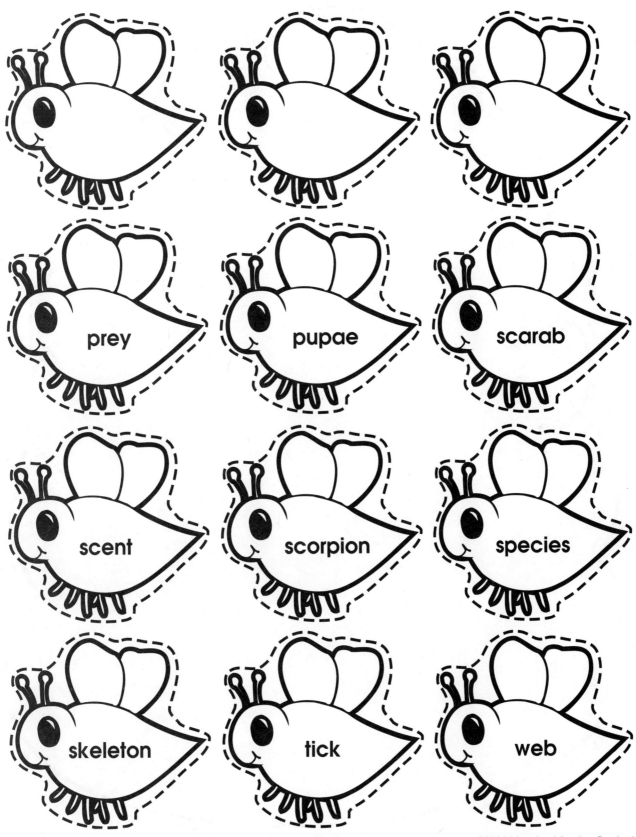

prey

pupae

scarab

scent

scorpion

species

skeleton

tick

web

Hive Pattern

Award Winners

Charlotte (the star of *Charlotte's Web*) was an extremely talented spider. She could write words in her web. Many real-life bugs (and spiders) have incredible talents as well. For example:

- Lightning bugs have their own built-in lanterns. They can be greenish, yellowish, or reddish. The fireflies that give the brightest light live in South America. (lighting)
- Crickets create their own orchestras. (music)
- A bee knows how to give directions. (choreography/dance)
- A mosquito's wings beat 300 times a second. (stunts)
- One South American butterfly has bright yellow "scent scales" that help to attract the females. (special effects)

Materials:
"Award Winners" Hands-on Handout (p. 44), "Insect A to Z List" (p. 78), "Super-Duper Fact Cards" (pp. 70-77), "Award Patterns" (p. 45), crayons or markers, tape, scissors

Directions:
1. Duplicate the "Award Winners" Hands-on Handout for each child in the classroom.
2. Let each child choose an insect to research. (You can let them choose from the "Insect A to Z List.") Children can research their chosen insect using the "Super-Duper Fact Cards," or by using library books.
3. Have each child learn one to three impressive facts about their insect to recite to the rest of the class.
4. Hold an award show in your classroom. Duplicate the "Award Patterns," and let children award each other's insects.
5. Post the completed pictures with the awards on an "Award-Winning Insects" bulletin board.

Award Winners

What You Do:
1. Choose a creature to research. Write the name of your insect, spider, or creepy crawly here:

_____

2. Research your insect and write down three facts about it:

a) _____

_____

b) _____

_____

c) _____

_____

3. Draw a simple picture of your insect.

4. Pick a super fact to tell to the class.
5. When your classmates give your insect awards, tape or glue them to the border of your picture.
6. Give your picture to your teacher to post on a bulletin board.

Award Patterns

Best
Lighting

Best
Sound

Best
Special
Effects

Best Dancing

Best
Stunts

Charlotte's Web

Story:

Charlotte's Web by E. B. White, illustrated by Garth Williams (Harper, 1952).

Charlotte's Web may be named for Charlotte the spider, but it actually tells the tale of Wilbur the pig. Wilbur is destined to become someone's dinner until Charlotte, an amiable arachnid, comes to the rescue. Her spinning antics draw a crowd to the farm, create quite a day for the press, and save Wilbur's life. That swell pig has "some swell" friend in Charlotte! (This story is also available on videotape.)

Setting the Stage:

- Create the feel of a country fair in your classroom by cutting ribbon shapes from blue construction paper and using these as name tags, hall passes, or desk or cubby labels for your students.
- Draw a simple web on the corner of the chalkboard and write a different spelling word in the center every day of the week.
- Hold a "farm day" at school, and have children dress accordingly: encourage overalls and bandannas.
- Serve cups of lemonade for an early afternoon snack.

Tricky Tongue Twister:

Silly spiders spin super sticky silky string.

Words in a Web

Charlotte uses her spinnerets to save Wilbur's life. She writes messages in the web, such as "Some Swell Pig" and "Incredible!"

Materials:
Black construction paper, silver crayons, silver glitter, glue

Directions:
1. Have the children imagine that they are arachnid authors.
2. Provide silver crayons for them to use to write important messages on black paper. They can pretend to be Charlotte writing messages to save Wilbur's life. Or they can write notes to their friends, or to other insects.
3. Children can further decorate their messages with glitter and glue to create shimmering spider webs.
4. Post the finished pictures on a "Some Swell Spiders" bulletin board.

Note:
If silver crayons are hard to find, provide black crayons to be used on white paper.

Option:
Decorate the bulletin board with plastic spider rings dangling from silver ribbons. These rings are usually very affordable right after Halloween and can be found at party, craft, and novelty stores.

Anansi the Spider

Story:

Anansi the Spider: A Spider Tale from the Ashanti by Gerald McDermott (Holt, 1972).
This story spins the tale of Anansi, who is a very different kind of spider than that do-gooder Charlotte. Anansi is a famous spider from Africa. Stories have been told about him for many years because he is fun to hear about. Anansi uses very creative methods to trick the other animals.

Setting the Stage:

- Locate Africa on a classroom map or globe.
- Anansi the Spider Man wears cool threads. Have a hat-wearing day and encourage children to wear their favorite hat to school. (If this is not allowed at your school, have children wear neat scarves, ties, or ribbons.)
- Use yellow and green crepe paper to create the look of grasses on your walls.

Tricky Tongue Twister:

Web weaving's wearying work.

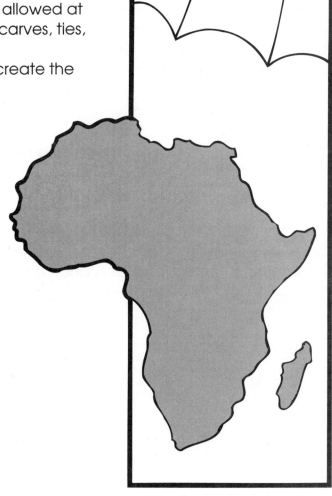

Tricky, Tricky

Materials:
Construction paper in a variety of colors, spider patterns (bottom of this page), scissors, crayons or markers, glue, tape, leaves and twigs (optional)

Directions:
1. Let each child choose a sheet of colored construction paper for a background.
2. Duplicate the spider patterns for each child to color and cut out.
3. Have the children glue their colored spider patterns to the construction paper.
4. Children can use crayons, markers, and construction paper scraps to create camouflage scenes for their spiders. They can hide larger spiders beneath taped-on leaves, or glue the tiny spiders to the edges of a glued-on branch.
5. Post the "Tricky, Tricky" pictures on a bulletin board and have the children try to find the spiders in each one.

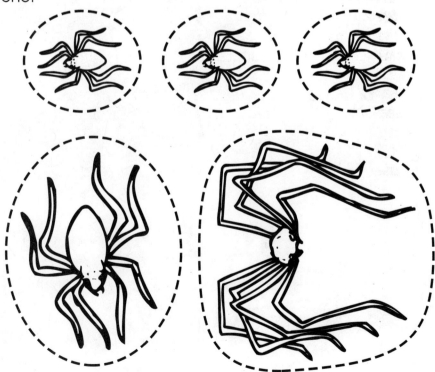

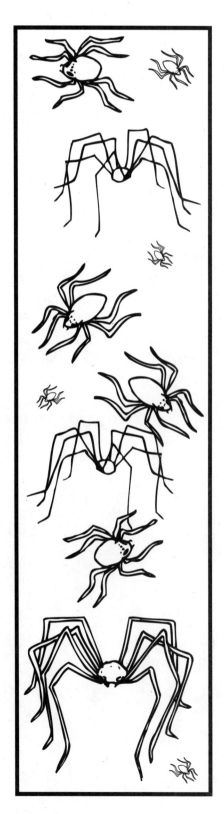

James and the Giant Peach

Story:

James and the Giant Peach by Roald Dahl, illustrated by Nancy Ekholm Burkert (Knopf, 1989).
Young James lives a miserable life with his two awful aunts. Happily, his luck changes when he meets a mysterious stranger who gives him magic green "stones." These stones (actually thousands of wriggly crocodile tongues) are the key to an exciting adventure on a giant peach! Along for the ride are a few giant insects, including a cricket and a ladybug.

Setting the Stage:

- Create an ocean setting by cutting wave shapes from blue construction paper. Post these along the walls of the classroom.
- Draw a giant peach on the chalkboard using pale pink chalk. When you get to the part in the story where sharks begin to eat the peach, children can erase "bites" from the drawing.
- Bring a flashlight to class and read a few pages by its light. (Read the pages that describe when James first arrives on the peach. Then, when the centipede tells the glowworm to turn out her light, you can turn off the flashlight.)
- Serve Peachy Punch: peach nectar mixed with ginger ale or 7-up.

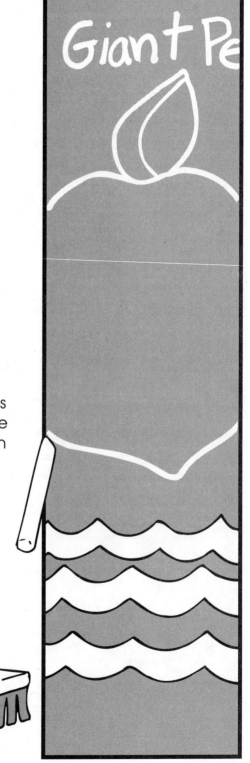

The Luck of the Bug

Materials:
Drawing paper, crayons

Directions:
1. Tell the children that common ladybugs have seven spots. Some people consider ladybugs to be lucky, so have the children imagine that each spot is worth a wish.
2. Provide drawing paper and crayons for children to use to draw lucky, seven-dotted ladybugs. Have them make the dots large and round—they should not color in the dots.
3. Have the children write a wish in each of their ladybug's spots.
4. Post the completed wish pictures on a "Buggy Luck" bulletin board.

Option:
For a decorative background, cover the board with shiny red construction paper and glue on black construction paper dots.

Lady Bugatti

Story:

Lady Bugatti by Joyce Maxner, illustrated by Kevin Hawkes (Lothrop, Lee & Shepard, 1991).
Lady Bugatti is a classy ladybug who throws a beautiful dinner party for her friends. After dinner, the guests drive with Lady Bugatti to the theater, where she surprises them all by performing on stage! Destined to be a classic, *Lady Bugatti* is told in rhyme.

Setting the Stage:

- Lady Bugatti invites all of her friends to dinner. Her friends have very interesting names. Have the children write their own names with a buggy flair: Fiona Firefly, Lorenzo Ladybug, Peter Praying Mantis, Cara Cockroach, and so on. Refer to the "Insect A to Z List" on p. 78. Children can write their "new names" on a ladybug-shaped desk label.
- Host a fancy-dress day. Have children wear their favorite dress-up clothes. (They can bring them to school in bags for protection and put them on after lunch.)

Tricky Tongue Twister:

Ladybugs are beetle beauties.

Ladybug Rhyme Time

Materials:
Writing paper, pencils

Directions:
1. After reading *Lady Bugatti*, challenge your students to create buggy rhymes of their own.
2. Write the names of common bugs on the board (refer to the "Insect A to Z List" on page 78).
3. Have the children brainstorm rhyming words. You can start them off with the following examples:

- bug: chug, dug, lug, mug
- fly: by, high, my, sty
- roach: coach, poach
- ant: can't, chant, pant, plant
- flea/bee: me, tree, be, sea

4. Have children string together simple rhymes. For example:
The flea in the tree saw me.

More advanced students can take the rhymes further:
I saw the flea in the tree.
The flea in the tree saw me.
He saw me, I saw he.
We saw we.

The Cricket in Times Square

Story:

The Cricket in Times Square by George Selden, illustrated by Garth Williams (Farrar, 1960).

A cricket named Chester spends one summer in New York City (where he is transported in someone's picnic basket). The tiny creature finds three really good friends: a little boy named Mario whose parents run an unsuccessful newsstand in the subway station at Times Square, a fast-talking Broadway mouse named Tucker, and Harry the Cat. Mario believes that crickets are good luck.

Setting the Stage:

- Create the feel of a newsstand by bringing in a variety of papers and magazines and displaying them on a low table in the classroom. Children can pretend to buy and sell the papers to each other.
- Play a tape recording of cricket sounds—available at many science stores or teacher supply stores.
- Set up a buffet (like Harry and Tucker did) and play music to go with it.
- Host an amateur singing hour like the one Harry, Tucker, and Chester participated in after their dinner party.

Tricky Tongue Twister:

"Clickety, clackety!" cried the cricket.

Creating a Cricket Pagoda

In *The Cricket in Times Square*, Mario keeps Chester in a matchbox until a friend tells him that the Chinese keep crickets in special cricket houses.

Materials:
Small milk cartons (cleaned and dried; one per child), construction paper, glue, scissors, glitter, sequins, buttons, cricket patterns (on the bottom of this page), crayons or markers

Directions:
1. Give each child a small milk carton to decorate like a cricket pagoda.
2. Children can use scissors to cut out doors in their cricket houses.
3. Provide construction paper and glue for children to use to decorate the pagodas.
4. Extra decorations, such as glitter, sequins, and buttons, can also be used to further decorate the pagodas.
5. Duplicate the cricket patterns and give one to each child to color and keep in the cricket pagoda.

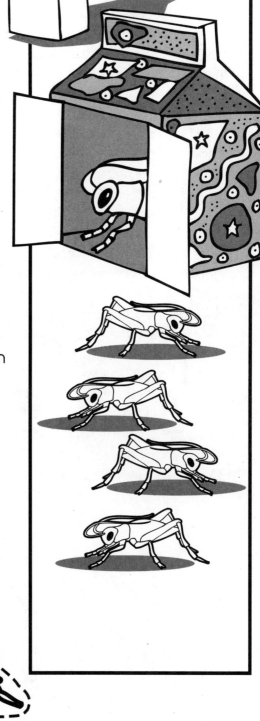

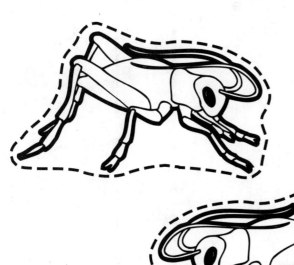

Quick As a Cricket

Story:

Quick As a Cricket by Audrey Wood, illustrated by Don Wood (Child's Play, 1982).
This book is filled with comparisons, such as "quick as a cricket," "nice as a bunny," "quiet as a clam," and so on. Don Wood creates beautiful images that fit the text perfectly.

Setting the Stage:

- Post on a wall or bulletin board pictures of different animals cut from nature magazines. Beneath the pictures, write partially completed similes. For example, under a bunny, write "_____ as a bunny" and under a turtle write "_____ as a turtle." Post blank sheets of paper beneath the comparison set-ups and let children create lists of words that fill in the blanks, for example, "slow, old, green" as a turtle.

- Discuss adjectives by hosting a self-description day. Give each child a blank sticker (the name tag type worn at conventions works well). Have each child write a word (or words) on the sticker that describes their feelings that day. Write a list of words on the board to give them a start: happy, silly, angry, beautiful, talented, hot, cold, and so on.

Tricky Tongue Twister:

The cricket's so quick, he goes lickety-split.

Compared to a Cricket

Materials:
Writing paper, pencils

Directions:
1. Have your children choose an insect to compare themselves to, a cricket, for example.
2. At the top of a piece of paper, have each child write, "Compared to a..." (and list the insect of choice).
3. Have the children brainstorm ways they are alike and different from the insect they've chosen. For example, "Compared to a cricket, I am very big." "Compared to an ant, I have a very small family." "Compared to a bee, I eat a lot of different foods."
4. Bind the completed papers in a classroom book.

Extension:
Children can do this activity based on observations they've made or facts they already know. Or, have children research an insect and compare/contrast themselves to it based on the facts they find out.

Writing a Famous Bug Story

Materials:

"Famous Bug Stories" Hands-on Handout (p. 59), crayons or markers, writing paper, pencils or markers, drawing paper, hole punch and yarn (for binding)

Directions:

1. Challenge your students to think of famous spiders and bugs. Here are a few to start them off (you can write the list on the chalkboard and add any names that the children think up):

- Charlotte the Spider
- Spider Man (the comic)
- Anansi the Spider
- Jiminy Cricket (star of "Pinocchio")
- The Fly Who Was Swallowed by the Little Old Lady
- The Moth in "Dr. Doolittle"
- The Fly (in the horror movie of the same name)

2. Next, have each child create a famous bug or spider story, following the simple directions on page 59.
3. When the children have finished their stories, have them illustrate one scene from their tales.
4. Bind the completed stories and pictures in a classroom book, or post the pictures and stories side by side in a hallway display that the whole school can enjoy.

Famous Bug Stories

What You Do:

1. Choose a type of bug to write about.
2. Name your bug. (You can choose a human name and add the type of insect as a "last name," for example, Bert the Bedbug or Wilma Waterbug. Or choose a name that has something to do with the type of bug it is: A Bee Called Buzz.)
3. Describe the way your bug looks.
4. Think about reasons why your bug could be famous:
   • Is it a crime fighter?
   • Can it do tricks?
   • Does it eat a lot?
   • Can it read and write?
5. Write a short story about your famous bug. Begin with an exciting event. In *James and the Giant Peach*, James is given a bag of green objects.
6. Draw a picture of your bug (making sure to use the correct number of eyes, legs, wings, and so on).

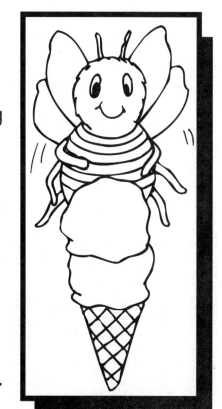

7. Read your story aloud, then show your picture.

Incredible Insects Program

Songs:
- Oh, My Darling Centipede
- Do You Like to Buzz?
- Oh, Look, There's a Bee
- A Cricket Is Quite a Musician
- The Caterpillar Song
- The Monarch Song
- Grasshopper Hop
- A Firefly Has Its Own Night Light

Featuring:

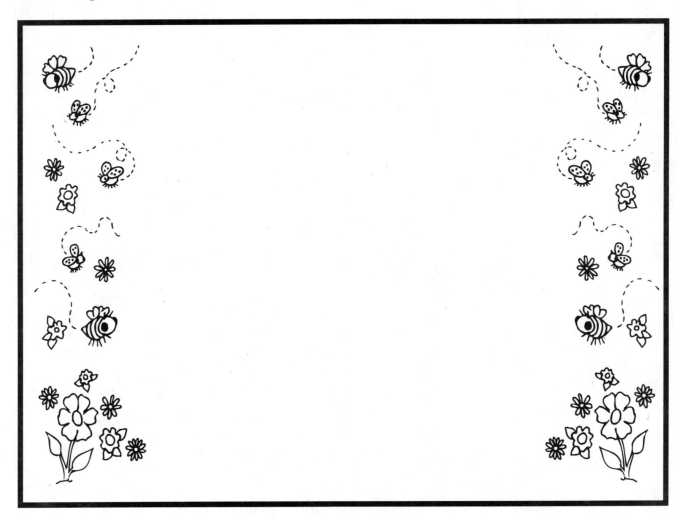

Oh, My Darling Centipede

(to the tune of "Clementine")

Oh, my darling,
Oh, my darling,
Oh, my darling centipede.
Buying shoes must be a hassle
When you've got seventy feet.

Buying sneakers, for those tootsies,
It must make you frown and pout.
I will help you lace your tennies
When you're ready to go out.

Oh, my darling,
Oh, my darling,
Oh, my darling centipede.
Buying shoes must be a hassle
When you've got seventy feet.

Centipede Costume

What You Need:

What You Do:
1. Cut arm slits on the sides of the bag and a circle for your head to fit through.
2. Paint the bag using tempera paint.
3. While the bag is drying, cut construction paper into strips. These will be your centipede's legs.
4. Cut out the sneaker shape on this page. Use it to trace sneakers onto colored construction paper and cut them out. Make as many legs and sneakers as you want.
5. Tape or glue one sneaker to one end of each construction paper strip.
6. Attach the free end of each strip to the paper bag costume using glue or tape.
7. Slip on the costume and get ready to sing. When you move, your "legs" will bounce and move, too.

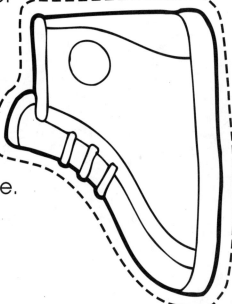

Do You Like To Buzz?

(to the tune of "Do Your Ears Hang Low?")

**Do you like to buzz?
Are you covered with black fuzz?
Do you know how to make honey?
(Are your stripes a little funny?)
Do you call a hive your home,
In the garden, where you roam?
Do you like to buzz?**

Oh, Look, There's a Bee

(to the tune of "Oh, Give Me a Home")

**Oh, look, there's a bee,
And it's following me,
It must think I'm a flower in bloom.
But I don't agree,
I'm no flower—just me,
Still I'll move just to give him some room.**

**Bee, don't follow me.
I don't smell like a flower or tree.
It's pollen you sniff,
Go ahead, take a whiff,
And then fly on your way, that's my plea.**

Bee Costume

What You Need:

Curl

What You Do:

1. Cut arm slits on the sides of the bag and a circle for your head to fit through.
2. Paint alternating black and yellow stripes along the bag horizontally.
3. While the bag dries, take a strip of black construction paper and wrap it around your head to make a headband. Size the strip, then tape the ends together to make a loop. (It should slide on comfortably, then stay in place.)
4. Staple two pipe cleaners to the headband and curl the free edges around your finger. This will be your antennae.
5. Once the body of your costume is dry, slide it on. Then add your antennae, and get ready to sing!

A Cricket Is Quite a Musician

(to the tune of "My Bonnie Lies Over the Ocean")

A cricket is quite a musician.
It uses its legs to play tunes.
At twilight I sit down and listen
To concerts played under the moon
    (the moon).
Cricket, oh, cricket,
Won't you play a new song for me?
    (for me?)
Cricket, oh, cricket,
Won't you play a new song for me?

Note: Wear black or dark clothing while you sing this song.

The Caterpillar Song

(to the tune of "Take Me Out to the Ball Game")

Munch and munch on the flowers,
Eat some nice crinkly leaves,
Wrap yourself up in a tight cocoon,
Where you'll stay 'til May or 'til June,
And then warm your wings in the sunshine,
And sit on a leaf, way up high.
What a lovely creature you are,
Mr. Butterfly!

The Monarch Song

(to the tune of "Take Me Out to the Ball Game")

You hatched out of a small egg,
Munched upon many leaves.
You grew your legs at a speedy rate,
With all those legs you will never be late!
Then you wrapped yourself up in silk threads
And dreamed of soaring so high,
And we watched you lose your cocoon,
Monarch butterfly!

Butterfly Wings

What You Need:

What You Do:

1. Cut out large wing shapes from the butcher paper. (Trace the wing shapes ahead of time with a pencil. You'll be making a double-heart shape, without the point.)

2. Cut two 10" strips from the construction paper.

3. Tape one strip to the inside of each wing. Place a piece of tape at either end. (These are your arm straps. You'll slip your arms through them to wear your wings.)

4. Turn the wings over and paint them with your choice of tempera paint. You can draw actual butterfly designs that you've seen in books, or create your own butterfly-wing pattern.

5. Wear your wings when you sing the butterfly songs.

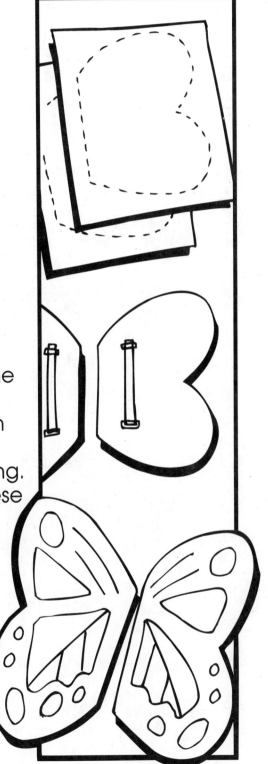

Grasshopper Hop

(to the tune of "Jingle Bell Rock")

Grasshopper, grasshopper, grasshopper hop,
Grasshopper's green, he rarely is seen.
Hopping on grass blades, and jumping on sticks—
What a fancy trick!

When you're outside, in a meadow,
Take a look all around—
'Cause a hopper's hard to pick out,
He blends in with hardly a sound.

Grasshopper, grasshopper, grasshopper hop,
Grasshopper jump, and grasshopper glide.
Hopping from grass stems and skipping on sticks—
What a fancy trick!

Note: Wear green while you sing "Grasshopper Hop."

A Firefly Has Its Own Night Light

(to the tune of "My Bonnie Lies Over the Ocean")

A firefly has its own night light,
It blinks on and off as it flies.
The light is this bug's way of talking
To all of its pals in the sky, the sky.

Lightning bug, lightning bug,
Turn on your bright light for me, for me.
Lightning bug, lightning bug,
Turn on your bright light for me!

Note: Wear black while you perform this song, and flash a flashlight on and off.

Ant Facts

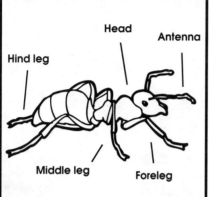

Habitat: Ants live in colonies, or groups, of 100,000 or more. They can be found in deserts, woods, fields, and gardens.
Food: Ants eat honeydew that is made by aphids.
Enemies: The anteater is an enemy.
Way of "talking": Ants touch each other to pass on the smell of their nest.

Super-Duper Fact: Ants are able to lift objects that weigh more than they do!

Aphid Facts

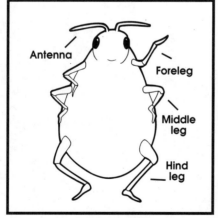

Habitat: Aphids live in house plants and home gardens.
Food: Aphids like to eat roses, beans, cabbages, and other plants.
Enemies: The ladybug is their main enemy.
Camouflage: Aphids are usually green. This helps them blend with the stems and leaves of plants.

Super-Duper Fact: Aphids have spear-like mouths that help them to drink sap from plants.

Bee Facts

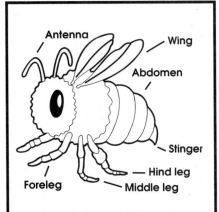

Antenna
Wing
Abdomen
Stinger
Hind leg
Middle leg
Foreleg

Habitat: A beehive can be home to more than 50,000 bees.
Food: Bees suck nectar with their tube-shaped mouth parts.
Way of "talking": A worker bee "dances" by waggling her abdomen. This is how she tells other bees where the nectar is.
Queen Bee: The queen bee spends her life laying eggs.
Super-Duper Fact: A bee can use its stinger only once.

Beetle Facts

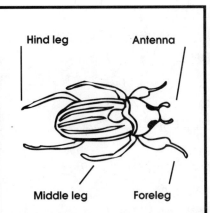

Hind leg
Antenna
Middle leg
Foreleg

Habitat: Beetles can be found on mountains, in deserts, and in ponds.
Food: Some beetles eat only vegetables. Underwater beetles eat tadpoles.
Enemies: Birds and fish are two beetle enemies.
Number of babies: The Mexican bean beetle lays her eggs in groups of about 50.
Super-Duper Fact: The scarab was a sacred beetle in ancient Egypt.

Butterfly Facts

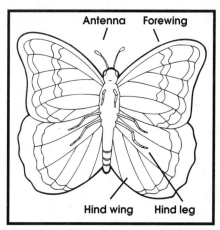

Antenna   Forewing

Hind wing   Hind leg

Habitat: Butterflies live in grasslands, mountains, and rain forests.
Food: Butterflies eat liquid nectar from flowers.
Enemies: Birds and lizards are two of their enemies.
Way of "talking": Butterflies use sight and smell to find their mates.

Super-Duper Fact: Some butterflies use their front pair of legs for cleaning their eyes rather than for walking.

Centipede Facts

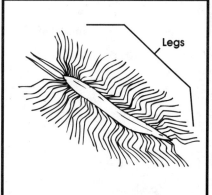

Legs

Habitat: Centipedes can be found in caves, deserts, forests, and gardens.
Food: Centipedes eat insect larva, slugs, snails, and worms. Large centipedes eat mice, birds, and lizards.
Enemies: Certain birds and ants eat centipedes, but most centipedes taste bad.

Super-Duper Fact: Most centipedes have 35 pairs of legs. (Centipedes are not insects—insects have only six legs!)

Cockroach Facts

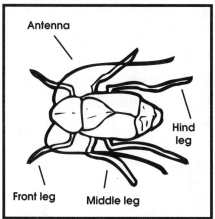

Antenna

Hind leg

Front leg   Middle leg

Habitat: Cockroaches can live almost anywhere, but they like places with food...like kitchens.
Food: Cockroaches eat food, dirt, paper, or leather.
Way of "talking": Cockroaches drag the spurs at the ends of their legs on the ground to make noise.
Number of babies: Cockroaches lay 30 or 40 eggs at a time.

Super-Duper Fact: Cockroaches lay their eggs in an egg purse called an ootheca. It contains two rows of eggs.

Cricket Facts

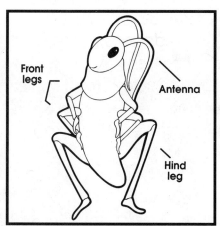

Front legs

Antenna

Hind leg

Habitat: Different types of crickets can be found in caves, houses, fields, trees, and underground.
Food: Crickets eat flowers, plants, and other insects.
Enemies: Bats and owls are two cricket enemies.
Way of "talking": Males "sing" by rubbing their front wings together.

Super-Duper Fact: A cricket can work as a thermometer! Count how many chirps the cricket makes in 15 seconds. Then add 39 to find the temperature.

Firefly Facts

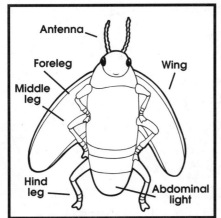

Labels: Antenna, Foreleg, Middle leg, Wing, Hind leg, Abdominal light

Habitat: Fireflies live in fields, woods, and backyards.
Food: They eat soft insects, worms, and snails when they are larva.
Way of "talking": Fireflies flash the lights in their tails to "talk" to each other.
Bright babies: Baby fireflies glow, too.

Super-Duper Fact: A chemical reaction in the firefly causes its tail to light up.

Grasshopper Facts

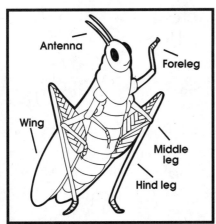

Labels: Antenna, Foreleg, Wing, Middle leg, Hind leg

Habitat: Grasshoppers live in mountains and deserts.
Food: They eat plants.
Enemies: Birds, spiders, and lizards are enemies.
Way of "talking": Grasshoppers rub their legs on their bodies to "talk" to each other.
Number of babies: They lay 20-120 eggs at a time.

Super-Duper Fact: Nymphs, young grasshoppers, eat twice their body weight in a day.

Ladybug Facts

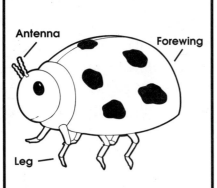

Habitat: Ladybugs can be found in fields and gardens.
Food: They love to eat aphids. One ladybug can eat 100 aphids in a day. Ladybugs help people by eating many harmful insects.
Enemies: Birds are one of their enemies.

Super-Duper Fact: Not all ladybugs are ladies. Males are called ladybugs, too!

Praying Mantis Facts

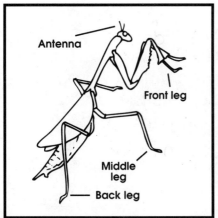

Habitat: Praying mantises like to live in warm or tropical climates.
Food: Praying mantises eat insects, frogs, lizards, and small birds.
Number of babies: Female mantises lay eggs in capsules or sacs. Each capsule contains 200 eggs. (One female might lay five capsules a year.)
Super-Duper Fact: There are 1,800 kinds of mantises.

Spider Facts

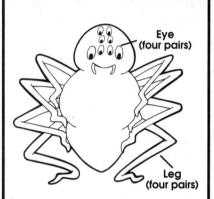

Eye
(four pairs)

Leg
(four pairs)

Habitat: Spiders can be found all over the world.
Food: Spiders eat insects, which they trap in their sticky webs.
Enemies: Birds eat spiders.
Way of "talking": Spiders are good listeners. They can tell the size of their enemies by the sounds they make.

Super-Duper Fact: Spiders use their silk for binding prey and making webs and cocoons.

Stinkbug Facts

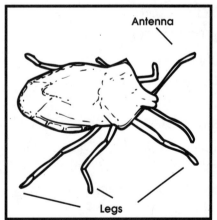

Antenna

Legs

Habitat: Stinkbugs can be found around the world, including Australia and Asia.
Food: They eat fruits and plants.
Enemies: Spiders, birds, frogs, mice, and ants eat stinkbugs.
Baby bugs: Stinkbug moms protect their eggs and young with a "shield" that covers their hindquarters.
Super-Duper Fact: Some stinkbugs can squirt smelly liquid.

Termite Facts

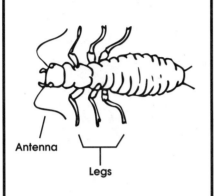

Antenna

Legs

Habitat: Termites are a worldwide pest. They live in damp wood.
Food: Termites have tiny creatures living in their stomachs that help them digest the wood.
Housing: Termites can build 40-foot (12.2m) mounds for housing. They live in groups of hundreds or thousands.

Super-Duper Fact: Termites will sometimes eat the wooden structure of a house and leave just the thin painted surface. They weaken wooden furniture and buildings.

Treehopper Facts

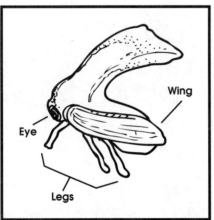

Wing

Eye

Legs

Habitat: Treehoppers live in gardens. The horned treehopper lives in Florida. Leafhoppers are relatives of treehoppers.
Food: They suck the juice from plants, which makes them a pest to gardeners.
Tree-top babies: Treehoppers lay their eggs inside the bark of trees.

Super-Duper Fact: Treehoppers look like the plants they live on.

Insect A to Z List

A: Ant, Aphid
B: Beetle, Brush-Snouted Weevil, Bumblebee
C: Caterpillar
D: Damselfly, Dragonfly
E: Earwig
F: Flat-Faced Katydid, Flea, Fly
G: Giant Australian Stick, Glowworm
H: Harlequin Bug, Horsefly
I: Imperial Moth
J: Jeweled Frog Beetle
K: Katydid
L: Ladybug
M: Malayan Leaf Insect
N: Nemoptera, Net-Winged Beetle
O: Oriental Cockroach
P: Praying Mantis, Peanut-Head Bug
Q: Queen Victoria's Birdwing
R: Robber Fly
S: Scorpion (arachnid), Shield Stinkbug
T: Tarantula (arachnid)
U: Urania Moth
V: Violet Beetle
W: Weevil
X: Xanthabraxas
Y: Yellow Jacket
Z: Zygaena

Nonfiction Resources

• *A First Look At Insects* by Millicent E. Selsam and Joyce Hunt, illustrated by Harriett Springer (Walker, 1974).

• *Animal Camouflage: A Closer Look* by Joyce Powzyk (Bradbury, 1990). Shows both insects and other animals.

• *Beetles* by Barrie Watts (Franklin Watts, 1989).

• *Beetles and How They Live* by Dorothy Hinshaw Patent and Paul C. Schroeder (Holiday House, 1978). This book discusses beetle foods and feeding, wings and flight, and much more.

• *Bug Wise* by Pamela M. Hickman, illustrated by Judie Shore (Ontario Naturalists, 1990).

• *Camouflage in the Wild: Hiding Out* by James Martin, photos by Art Wolfe (Crown, 1993). Shows insects as well as other animals.

• *Collecting Cocoons* by Lois J. Hussey and Catherine Pessino, illustrated by Isabel Sherwin Harris (Crowell, 1953).

• *Discovering Centipedes & Millipedes* by Ken Preston-Mafham (Bookright Press, 1990).

• *Entomology* by Ellen Doris, photographs by Len Rubenstein (Thames and Hudson, 1993). Includes detailed glossary that is very helpful.

• *Eyewitness Books: Insect* by Laurence Mound (Knopf, 1990). Includes chapters on the parts of an insect, metamorphosis, camouflaging, and more.

• *Grasshoppers* by Jane Dallinger, photographs by Yuko Sato (Lerner, 1981).

• *Hop, Skim, and Fly; An Insect Book* by Ross E. Hutchins (Parents Magazine Press, 1970).

• *How Insects Communicate* by Dorothy Hinshaw Patent (Holiday House, 1975).

• *Insect Metamorphosis: From Egg to Adult* by Ron and Nancy Goor (Atheneum, 1990). Insects grow in stages, not continuously the way people do. This book explains the stages of development.

• *Insects* by John Bonnett Wexo (Creative Education, 1989).

©1996 Monday Morning Books, Inc.

• *Insects All Around Us* by Richard Armour, illustrated by Paul Galdone (McGraw-Hill, 1981).
• *Insects in Armor: A Beetle Book* by Ross E. Hutchins, illustrated with photos by the author (Parents' Magazine Press, 1972).
• *Ladybugs* by Sylvia A. Johnson, photographs by Yuko Sato (Lerner, 1983).
• *The Life Cycle of a Grasshopper* by Jill Bailey, illustrated by Carolyn Scrace (Wayland, 1989). This informative resource has a very helpful glossary.
• *Monarch Butterfly* by Gail Gibbons (Holiday House, 1989).
• *The Moon of the Monarch Butterflies* by Jean Craighead George, illustrated by Murray Tinkelman (Crowell, 1968).
• *Termites* by Peter R. Limburg, illustrated by Kenneth Francis Dewey (Hawthorne Books, 1974).
• *The Travels of Monarch X* by Ross E. Hutchins, illustrated by Jerome P. Connolly (Rand McNally, 1966). This book tells the true story of a Monarch butterfly. This Monarch flew southward across the United States and on to Mexico, where it was recaptured.
• *What Bit Me?* by D. M. Souza (Carolrhoda, 1991).
• *What Is an Insect?* by Robert Snedden, photographs by Oxford Scientific Films, illustrated by Adrian Lascom (Sierra Club Books for Children, 1992).
• *Where Do They Go? Insects in Winter* by Millicent E. Selsam, illustrated by Arabelle Wheatley (Four Winds Press, 1982).
• *Where's That Insect?* by Barbara Brenner and Bernice Chardiet, illustrated by Carol Schwartz (Scholastic, 1993).